From Like to Love
for Young People with Asperger's Syndrome (Autism Spectrum Disorder)

by the same author

The Complete Guide to Asperger's Syndrome
Tony Attwood
ISBN 978 1 84310 495 7 (hardback)
ISBN 978 1 84310 669 2 (paperback)
eISBN 978 1 84642 559 2

Asperger's Syndrome
A Guide for Parents and Professionals
Tony Attwood
Foreword by Lorna Wing
ISBN 978 1 85302 577 8
eISBN 978 1 84642 697 1

for professionals

Exploring Feelings for Young Children with High-Functioning
Autism or Asperger's Disorder
The STAMP Treatment Manual
Angela Scarpa, Anthony Wells and Tony Attwood
ISBN 978 1 84905 920 6
eISBN 978 0 85700 681 3

of related interest

Freaks, Geeks and Asperger Syndrome
A User Guide to Adolescence
Luke Jackson
Foreword by Tony Attwood
ISBN 978 1 84310 098 0
eISBN 978 1 84642 356 7

Raising Martians – from Crash-landing to Leaving Home
How to Help a Child with Asperger Syndrome or High-functioning
Autism
Joshua Muggleton
Foreword by Tony Attwood
ISBN 978 1 84905 002 9
eISBN 978 0 85700 523 6

'To me as a parent, this book is a godsend – clear, logical, easy to read and above all useful!

It addresses a fundamental problem which is of concern to many parents: How can we, in practical terms, help our children learn to express and communicate their emotions, especially when they reach their teenage years and beyond?

Grounded on a solid base of expertise, experience and compassionate understanding, the authors offer a clear, insightful, structured solution. The sessions described in the book are easy to understand and equally easy to implement. They will go a long way to help our young people with Asperger's syndrome (autism spectrum disorder) understand the "rules of the game" and thereby achieve a more level playing field.'

– Brenda Boyd, author of Parenting a Child with Asperger
Syndrome, Parenting a Teen or Young Adult with
Asperger Syndrome (Autism Spectrum Disorder) *and*
Appreciating Asperger Syndrome

'A million thanks to Attwood and Garnett for writing this illuminating and user-friendly book that will surely help caregivers teach adolescents with Asperger's syndrome how to recognize and share emotions and affection in positive, nourishing and healthy ways.'

– Liane Holliday Willey, EdD, author of Safety Skills for
Asperger Women: How to Save a Perfectly Good Female
Life, Pretending to be Normal: Living with Asperger's
Syndrome, Asperger Syndrome in Adolescence: Living
with the Ups, the Downs and Things in Between *and*
Asperger Syndrome in the Family: Redefining Normal

'This book is clear, concise and practical...in other words, it is a parent's dream. The book gives us usable information in a blessedly short book. I recommend this book for parents, caregivers and teachers. Tony is one of the world's most empathic and creative experts on those individuals on the higher end of the autism spectrum. Michelle's work is already known in Australia, and she is a rising global star.'

C. 1

From Like
to Love

for Young People
with Asperger's Syndrome
(Autism Spectrum Disorder)

Learning How to Express and Enjoy
Affection with Family and Friends

TONY ATTWOOD
AND MICHELLE GARNETT

Jessica Kingsley *Publishers*
London and Philadelphia

First published in 2013
by Jessica Kingsley Publishers
116 Pentonville Road
London N1 9JB, UK
and
400 Market Street, Suite 400
Philadelphia, PA 19106, USA

www.jkp.com

Copyright © Tony Attwood and Michelle Garnett 2013
Illustrations copyright © Kaiyee Tay 2013

Library of Congress Cataloging in Publication Data
Attwood, Tony.
  From like to love for young people with asperger's syndrome (autism spectrum disorder) : learning how to express
and enjoy affection with family and friends / Tony Attwood and Michelle Garnett.
      pages cm
  Includes bibliographical references.
  ISBN 978-1-84905-436-2 (alk. paper)
  1. Asperger's syndrome in children--Patients--Life skills guides. 2. Autistic children--Life skills guides. 3.
Autism in children--Psychological aspects. 4. Cognitive therapy for children. I. Garnett, Michelle. II. Title.
  RJ506.A9A8694 2013
  618.92'858832--dc23
                            2013010990

British Library Cataloguing in Publication Data
A CIP catalogue record for this book is available from the British Library

ISBN 978 1 84905 412 6
eISBN 978 0 85700 777 3

Printed and bound in Great Britain by Bell & Bain Ltd, Glasgow

Contents

Part 1

Introduction

1

Why children and adolescents who have Asperger's syndrome (autism spectrum disorder) need a programme to understand and express affection

Affection in childhood

Within our families and friendships, we expect there to be a mutually enjoyable, reciprocal and beneficial regular exchange of words and gestures that express affection. From infancy, our children enjoy and seek affection from us, and as they become toddlers they learn to recognize when we expect affection and therefore learn when to give affection.

One of the early signs used to diagnose an autism spectrum disorder (ASD) in an infant or child is a lack of appearing to be comforted by affection when distressed. As typical children mature, they have an intuitive understanding of the type, duration and degree of affection appropriate for each situation and person. Children under two years know that using words and gestures of affection is perhaps the most effective way to help someone who is sad to feel happy again.

Affection for a child with an ASD

Unfortunately, for some children with an ASD, a gesture of affection, such as a hug, may feel like an uncomfortable and restricting physical sensation; your child may have learned not to cry as a result, to avoid eliciting that 'squeeze' from you. Your child may also be confused as to why you respond to his or her distress with a hug. As an adult with Asperger's syndrome said, 'How does a hug solve the problem?' Sometimes hugs are perceived and enjoyed by children with an ASD as relaxing deep pressure rather than a gesture to help them to feel happier.

Young boys and girls with an ASD often seem to prefer to play with hard toys, such as plastic models of dinosaurs and metal vehicles, rather than soft toys that represent human characteristics and tend to elicit strong feelings of love and affection in typical children and even adults. Children with an ASD will often not share when playing with peers. For typical children, sharing an activity or toy is generally an indication of their liking for someone. A child who doesn't like to share may be perceived as unfriendly or as not liking the other child.

Children with an ASD may also not recognize the social conventions of affection; for example, your child might express and expect in return the same degree of affection with a teacher as they would with you. There are also gender differences in the expression of affection between friends, with typical girls anticipating that affection will be part of their play. The absence of affection in the play of a girl with an ASD can be a barrier to friendship, and appearing aloof or indifferent to the affection of peers can make it difficult for both girls and boys with an ASD to be included in social groups and develop friendships.

Levels of affection

In general, a child with an ASD may enjoy a very brief and low-intensity expression of affection but become confused or overwhelmed when greater levels of expression are experienced or expected. However, the reverse can also be the case. Some children with an ASD need almost excessive amounts of affection for reassurance or sensory experience, and frequently express affection that is too intense or immature. A child or adolescent with an ASD may not perceive the non-verbal signals and contextual cues in order to know when to stop showing affection, and this can lead to feelings of discomfort or embarrassment in the other person.

Affection for emotional repair

When you express your love for your ASD child, perhaps with an affectionate hug, his or her body may stiffen rather than relax to match and fold into your body shape. Your child may also not be soothed by your words and gestures of affection when he or she is distressed. When an expression of love and affection is rejected or is not effective, you may wonder what you can do to repair the distress or whether your son or daughter actually loves or even likes you. Because your ASD child rarely uses affectionate gestures and words, you may feel deprived of affection. A mother of a daughter with Asperger's syndrome said that her daughter's lack of affection to family members was 'basically breaking her father's heart, he's devastated'. Another parent said, 'It really hurts that you can't have the relationship you wanted.' If affection is not reciprocated, you may try to elicit a greater degree of affection by increasing the intensity and frequency of your expressions of affection. This can lead to even greater withdrawal and mutual despair. Another characteristic often seen in children with an ASD is having a strong attachment to one parent and only accepting and expressing affection with that one parent. This can lead to the other parent feeling rejected and jealous.

Capacity for affection

When it comes to expressing affection, children with an ASD have a limited vocabulary of actions and gestures, and these often lack subtlety and (in the case of adolescents) may be inappropriate or immature for their age. Their expression of affection and of liking or loving someone may be perceived by family members or friends as too little or too much – drought or flood. An adolescent with Asperger's syndrome explained, 'We feel and show affection, but not often enough, and at the wrong intensity.' Each person has a capacity for expressing and enjoying affection. For a typical person, this capacity can be thought of as a bucket; but for someone with an ASD, it is like a cup that is quickly filled and slow to empty. If you fill the affection cup to capacity, your child can feel saturated with affection and unable to return the same degree of (or sometimes any) affection.

Affection in adolescence

Teenagers with an ASD may not understand the value in an adolescent friendship of mutual exchanges of appreciation and affection, which range from liking to loving. Such teenagers may have learned a vocabulary of words and gestures to express affection when they were very young, and then not modified these as they matured and as their social situations changed. For example, they may invade personal space and not know which parts of a person's body are now inappropriate to touch. The teenager with an ASD may also not know how to progress beyond a reciprocal but platonic friendship, or how to express deeper feelings of affection. There can also be a problem when an adolescent with an ASD develops a 'crush' on a peer. The expression of interest and affection can be perceived as too intense, and the adolescent may not recognize the need for mutual consent or age-appropriate social conventions and boundaries.

Thoughts and feelings

Often, children and teenagers with an ASD find it difficult to reflect on their own thoughts and feelings, as well as the thoughts and feelings of others. (Psychologists use the term 'impaired

Theory of Mind' to describe this difficulty.) Thus, a friend or acquaintance's act of kindness may be misinterpreted as having a more significant meaning than was intended. The person with an ASD may assume that the other person's feelings of affection are reciprocal, and may persistently follow the other person, seeking further acts of kindness. This can result in allegations of stalking and the destruction of the friendship.

Typical adolescents have many friends to provide guidance on appropriate levels of affection in a friendship or a romantic relationship. Adolescents with an ASD can become increasingly aware of the expressions of affection that occur between their peers and the apparent enjoyment of sensory experiences between a boyfriend and girlfriend. Such relationships can be elusive for a teenager with an ASD, but there may be an intellectual and emotional curiosity and a longing to have similar experiences. The adolescent may seek information and guidance on expressing affection from other sources, such as television programmes, which tend to emphasize dramatic expressions of affection; or from pornography on the internet, which portrays age-inappropriate or illegal activity. Serious problems can arise if such behaviour is suggested or imitated with peers. Immature and naïve expressions of affection can be misinterpreted as indicating a desire for greater intimacy than intended. Particularly for girls, this can lead to accusations of 'leading someone on', and to serious and traumatic experiences.

Recognizing signals

Another concern for some adolescent males with an ASD is knowing when to stop expressing affection in a romantic relationship. Typical teenagers recognize the verbal and non-verbal signals – the 'amber' or 'red light' signals – that indicate there is no consent to continue. If these signals are not recognized, accusations of assault and subsequent legal implications may follow.

In their desire to be popular, adolescents with an ASD are vulnerable to being 'set up' by malicious peers. There have been instances when a young person with an ASD has been deliberately misinformed that someone is romantically interested in him or her. When this false assumption leads to unwelcome advances or suggestions, the adolescent is confused – and accused. In contrast, some adolescents with an ASD are confused by aspects of affection and almost develop a phobia of experiencing, or even seeing, expressions of affection. They are then perceived as prudish or puritanical.

This programme has been designed primarily for children from 8 to 13 years with an ASD and an intellectual ability within the normal range. However, young children and older adolescents with an ASD who are particularly immature may also benefit from the activities and strategies used in the programme.

Empathy

If your child with an ASD rarely expresses affection, especially in situations where affection is anticipated, people may think that he or she lacks empathy. You wonder why such an accusation would be made toward someone who may demonstrate many acts of kindness.

There are two problems that could make people feel this way. The first is your child's limited ability to read the subtle body language and contextual cues that indicate someone is feeling distressed. If these subtle signs are not perceived, the anticipated response of concern, compassion and affection will not ensue. Furthermore, your child may not know how to respond appropriately and may fear responding in the wrong way – it may feel safer to do nothing.

Second, young people with an ASD can express and enjoy feelings of genuine and deep love and compassion for someone, but usually by practical demonstration rather than words or gestures of affection such as a hug or a kiss. For example, if someone is distressed because an object has been damaged or broken, your child's first response might be to repair or replace the object. However, if the cause of distress is a broken heart, perhaps because someone has died, your child may not know what to do and may be frozen in uncertainty. Thus, he or she may not recognize that a gesture or words of affection are a quick, powerful and inexpensive emotional restorative for friends and family members.

Affection to repair feelings

We have found that the three most effective emotional repair strategies for someone with an ASD are being alone, being with animals, or engaging in a special interest. This may explain why a young person with an ASD may choose to leave alone or avoid someone who is distressed. Another response that can be perceived as uncaring or annoying and indicative of a lack of empathy is trying to engage in a conversation about a special interest. This is not a display of callousness; it is actually his or her way of showing compassion. In other words, if it makes me feel better, it must work for you.

People with an ASD seem able to relate to and express affection and love more easily to animals than people. Thus, you may observe that your child can, and frequently does, express affection for a pet to a level far greater than is expressed for you. This can lead to feelings of envy of the pet and resentment that your child can express love but not for you. From your child's perspective, human beings have complex needs, can deceive or tease, interrupt and prevent you from engaging in your preferred activities. In contrast, animals are loyal, respectful, predictable and so pleased to see you, and it is easy to make them feel happy. Cats are particularly popular. Tony has sometimes referred to cats as being autistic dogs! You may feel that your son's or daughter's response to affection is like that of a cat: it is enjoyed sometimes when your child is in a receptive mood, but at other times it is clearly and almost painfully indicative of discomfort, and that leads to you feeling rejected.

Frequency of affection

We anticipate compliments and frequent words or gestures of affection as a natural part of a relationship or friendship. For your child with an ASD, this can be perceived as repetitive, illogical and a waste of time. Once a statement has been made, why should it have to be repeated? A mother complained to her adolescent son that he never said he loved her. He became very annoyed and replied that he had said he loved her when he was six years old. Why would he need to say it again? Was she developing signs of Alzheimer's?

Sensory sensitivity and affection

It is important for you and other family members and friends to recognize one particular aspect of ASD that may affect your child's ability to enjoy and express affection, and that is hyper- or hypo-reactivity to sensory experiences. For example, if your child is hyper-sensitive to touch, even light touch on his or her skin is an extremely unpleasant sensory experience. This will obviously affect your child's enjoyment of and response to gestures of affection, such as touching his or her hand or arm during a conversation to emphasize a point or to express compassion.

Unanticipated touch (such as a pat on the back or a hug from behind) can elicit a startle response. A kiss can also be perceived as an unpleasant tactile sensation. When experiencing a hug, a person with an ASD can be hyper-aware of someone's perfume or body odour, perceiving it as an extremely unpleasant sensation which is best avoided. All this can explain why your child may avoid the more demonstrative members of your family.

2

Aims of the programme

Affection is essential for physical and mental health and an important means of initiating and maintaining friendships and relationships. Parents and specialists in autism spectrum disorders are increasingly recognizing that children and adults with an ASD need information and guidance in the understanding and expression of affection.

The aims of the programme are as follows:

1. To help your child discover how expressing and experiencing affection can improve friendships and relationships.

2. To help your child to identify not only his or her own comfort and enjoyment range for gestures, actions and words of affection, but also those of friends and family members.

3. To improve your child's range of expressions for liking and loving someone, appropriate to each relationship and situation.

4. To explain the challenges faced by your child in reading the signals that indicate when expressions of affection are needed and appreciated.

This programme was originally designed by Professor Tony Attwood and Dr Michelle Garnett, two experienced clinical psychologists in Brisbane, Australia, who have specialized in autism spectrum disorders for several decades.

Who can use this programme?

You can follow this programme at home with your child. The activities are fairly simple, so no prior training is required before starting the programme.

You could also take part in the programme with a small group of children with an ASD and their parents, so reference is sometimes made to group activities.

3

Cognitive Behaviour Therapy

Children and adolescents with an autism spectrum disorder (ASD), especially Asperger's syndrome, are usually referred for the psychological treatment of a mood disorder as a result of concerns regarding the intensity of anxiety, sadness and anger. However, from our extensive clinical experience, we would suggest that there is a fourth emotion that is of particular concern to parents – namely the ability to understand and express feelings of affection. Children and adolescents with an ASD are often not instinctive and intuitive in expressing their liking or love for someone, or in their understanding that family members and friends need regular expressions of affection.

The primary psychological treatment for intense emotions is Cognitive Behaviour Therapy (CBT), which has been developed and refined over several decades. Research shows that CBT is an effective treatment to change the way a person thinks about and responds to emotions, especially anxiety, sadness and anger. This is probably the first CBT programme to focus specifically on affection.

CBT focuses on the maturity, complexity, subtlety and vocabulary of emotions, and on dysfunctional or illogical thinking and incorrect assumptions. Thus, it is particularly helpful where children and adults with an ASD have impaired or delayed abilities and difficulty understanding, expressing and managing emotions. CBT is about:

- becoming more consciously aware of one's emotional state

- knowing how to respond to the emotion

- becoming more sensitive to how others are feeling

- knowing how to respond to the emotions of others. This can be particularly difficult for people with an ASD.

The premise of cognitive behaviour therapy (CBT) is that changing thinking and knowledge leads to a change in emotions and behaviour. The therapy helps the person challenge and change beliefs, assumptions and responses and decrease emotional distress as well as increase emotional enjoyment. CBT has four components or stages:

1. The first is an assessment of the nature and degree of the problem.

2. The second component aims to increase your child's knowledge of emotions. Through discussion and activities you will explore the connection between thoughts, emotions and behaviour, and identify the ways in which your child understands emotions and perceives various situations. The more your child understands emotions, the more he or she is able to express and control them appropriately.

3. The third stage of CBT aims to correct distorted thinking and to manage emotions constructively.

4. The last stage is a schedule of activities for practising new skills to comprehend and express emotions in real-life situations.

This programme includes all of these components.

CBT includes education in when and how to express emotions, and with what frequency, and the appropriate intensity for the particular person and situation. We have applied the strategies used in CBT to help your child to:

- understand the concept and feelings of affection in themselves and others

- change thinking and behaviour

- reduce the anxiety, confusion and frustration often associated with feelings of affection.

The intention is gradually to increase your child's tolerance and enjoyment of affection, as well as his or her ability and confidence in expressing affection, ranging from like to love in a friendship or within your family. Having learned to enjoy and accept affection, your child will be able to accept that he or she is personally likeable and lovable.

Even if your child feels confused about affection and its expression, he or she still has the very human need for approval, liking and love. Thus, as the new skills of affection are practised, your child is more likely to receive approval, liking and love in return. Feeling that he or she is liked and loved by friends and family leads your child to feel greater self-acceptance and self-confidence in social situations. Greater engagement in friendships and family becomes possible and provides important preparation for future relationships.

There is evidence that CBT can significantly reduce problems in the communication and expression of emotions in children and adults with an ASD. Although a CBT programme is usually implemented by a clinical psychologist, this programme has been designed to be implemented by parents and is thus accessible and jargon-free.

The neurology of affection

Research using neuro-imaging technology with people who have an ASD has identified structural and functional abnormalities of the amygdala, a part of the brain associated with the recognition and regulation of emotions. The amygdala is known to regulate a range of emotions including anger, anxiety, sadness and affection. Thus, we also have neuro-anatomical evidence to suggest that those who have an autism spectrum disorder may have problems with the perception and regulation of emotions, including affection.

Best-selling author and internationally recognized expert in autism, Temple Grandin, explained that:

> My brain scan shows that some emotional circuits between the frontal cortex and the amygdala just aren't hooked up – circuits that affect my emotions and are tied to my ability to feel love. I experience the emotion of love, but it's not the same way that most neurotypical people do. Does this mean my love is less valuable than what other people feel? (Grandin and Barron 2005, p.40)

Part 2

How the Programme Works

4

Assessing the ability to communicate affection

Questionnaires

When the original CBT programme for affection was being designed, we devised three measures of affection that could be used to explore the ability of typical children and adolescents, and those with an ASD, to communicate affection and to measure progress made during the programme (Sofronoff *et al.*, in press). The three questionnaires, which are in the Appendix of this book, are:

- *The Affection for Others Questionnaire*: This is a 20-item questionnaire that examines giving and receiving verbal and physical affection, and the communication of empathy by the child, to *classmates, friends* and *family members*.

- *The Affection for You Questionnaire*: A 19-item questionnaire that examines giving and receiving verbal and physical affection, and the communication of empathy by the child, to a *parent*.

- *The General Affection Questionnaire*: A 12-item questionnaire that examines aspects of affection communication such as expressing inadequate or excessive affection, the importance of affection in your child's daily life, and the degree to which teaching and support regarding affection are required.

Stories

After listening to each of the stories described below, your child is asked certain questions that relate to the communication of affection. The stories can help to assess your child's understanding of the purpose of affection. Read each scenario to your child and record his or her responses. The score for each story is obtained by allocating one point for each appropriate response. The 'A Walk in the Forest' test has been found to be a sensitive measure of change in the understanding of affection (Sofronoff *et al.* 2011).

The three stories are included in Sessions 1 and 5 in Part 3 of this book.

A Walk in the Forest

In this story your child imagines meeting an alien who has recently landed on planet Earth. Invite your child to explain to the alien why humans are affectionate towards each other. This can show your child's depth of understanding of the value of affection.

Returning Home from School

Ask your child to imagine returning from school to find Mum sitting at the kitchen table in tears, and evidently in great distress. Explain that her distress has nothing to do with her child, who is then asked what he or she would do in that situation. A first response is usually to ask, 'What is the matter?' or 'What has happened?' Then, more importantly, encourage your child to suggest what he or she would do or say to make Mum feel better. The answers indicate whether and how your child expresses affection, the type of affection (such as giving a hug), and whether there is a greater emphasis on practical means of emotion recovery, such as offering to do the washing-up or handing Mum a tissue.

A Friend Feeling Sad

Ask your child to imagine arriving at school just before his or her friend. The friend enters the school grounds looking very sad, and explains that early that morning his or her dog escaped from home, ran across a road, was hit by a car, and died. Ask your child what he or she would do in that situation to console the friend.

Pre- and post-programme assessment

Ideally, the three affection questionnaires and the three stories should be used before you begin the programme, as they will provide you with useful information about how your child communicates affection, and help you to understand the type of affection he or she uses in specific situations. The questionnaires and stories should also be used at the end of the programme to measure any changes in your child's concept of affection, and assess whether the way your child thinks about and expresses affection has altered following the programme.

5

How to conduct the sessions

Children and adolescents with an ASD are more responsive to programmes that are highly structured and appeal to the logical or scientific thinking associated with ASD. Their cognitive profile can include remarkable visual reasoning abilities, and the activities are therefore enhanced with the use of pictures and drawing, thereby placing less emphasis on conversation. Because children with an ASD often have problems with generalization and the recall of information in different situations, role plays and practice in real-life situations are important elements of the programme. You may also need to bear in mind other characteristics of people with an ASD – for example, the tendency to make literal interpretations, which means that that idioms and metaphor could be confusing.

The approach used in this programme appeals to the logical thinking of children and adolescents with an ASD. Due to their problems with Theory of Mind (the ability to reflect on the thoughts and feelings of other people as well as their own thoughts and feelings), there needs to be a greater component of the programme devoted to how to discover the salient cues that indicate specific thoughts and feelings, and how to perceive the various levels of affection from like to love within themselves and others. Strategies specifically designed for children with an ASD to improve Theory of Mind abilities are Social Stories™ and Comic Strip Conversations™, which have been developed by Carol Gray (see Recommended Resources).

Social Stories™ enable you to explore and understand the perspective of your child and discover together how he or she can express an appropriate level of affection in a specific situation. Social Stories™ also explain the value of expressing affection. For example, they can be used to explain why friends and family need frequent reminders that they are liked or loved, even if they have no reason to doubt there is genuine affection for that friend or family member.

Comic Strip Conversations™ use simple drawings with stick figures, and thought, speech and emotion bubbles to illustrate events and emotions. You can create a Social Story™ or use Comic Strip Conversations™ to supplement the designated activity within the session.

Another problem often experienced by children with an ASD is a diminished vocabulary to describe the different levels of emotional experience, especially for more subtle or complex emotions. The approach adopted in this programme aims to enable your child to express his or her degree of liking or loving someone using a thermometer or numerical rating to indicate the intensity of experience and enjoyment.

In Part 3 of the book there are worksheets for your child to record information, although this aspect is deliberately kept to a minimum since children with an ASD often have poor handwriting skills and prefer to listen, watch and do, rather than write. If your child has a genuine aversion to writing, you can listen to his or her spoken comments and answers and then write them on the worksheets. Readers have permission to photocopy all worksheets marked with a ✓ for personal use. They are also available to download from www.jkp.com/catalogue/book/9781849054362/resources.

At the end of each session the project to be completed before the next session is explained, and the information obtained from the project discussed at the start of the subsequent session. These projects are designed to obtain more information and to apply strategies in real situations. Your child may have an aversion to the concept of homework from bitter school experiences, so you need to emphasize the importance of completing the project and clearly encourage your child to do so. Good collaboration between home and school with regard to expressing affection to friends will be beneficial. Make sure that teachers are aware of the programme and ways in which they can contribute to your child's knowledge base on expressing and responding to affection with peers. Teachers can also help with the successful implementation of strategies.

Always emphasize success and discovery, acknowledging contributions and discouraging 'right' or 'wrong' answers. Always encourage positive suggestions from your child. Feel free to deviate from the prescribed text to accommodate your child, and use aspects of ASD to illustrate a point; for example, use the feelings of elation associated with a special interest as a metaphor for feeling love for someone. The duration of each activity is variable, according to the attention and learning capacity and rate of progress of your child; however, as a general guide, each session is designed to be covered within one hour. The activities do not have to be completed in the sequence they occur in the workbook, and you may include additional activities and resources. Thus, the programme is flexible in structure and duration, and can evolve to meet the needs of your child.

Fear of failure

Clinical experience has identified that children with an ASD may have an almost pathological fear of failure. Make an effort to encourage self-confidence, and explain to your child that not knowing something or making an error is not a disaster but an opportunity to learn and become wiser. It is important to positively reinforce your child's abilities throughout the programme.

Group sessions

If you are participating in the programme with other children and parents, there are some things to be aware of.

Participants

It is important to select participants carefully, as children and adolescents with an ASD are at risk of additional diagnoses, particularly ADHD and oppositional defiant disorder. The personality of each participant and his or her emotional and intellectual maturity will have an effect on group cooperation, mutual support and the possibility of the development of friendships within and after the group sessions. Reduce the potential for personality clashes and ensure an even distribution of support. Having a participant who requires extra supervision and explanations in comparison to other group members may impact the rate of progress and the success of the group.

Ideally you should conduct the programme with no more than two children per adult, as the content of the programme requires you to carefully observe the degree of engagement and comprehension of the participating children. If two adults conduct the programme with a group of four children, for example, one can lead each activity while the other maintains attention and records information.

Setting

There must also be some special consideration of the setting for the programme when conducted in a small group, with the provision of sufficient personal space and comfortable chairs, and an awareness of the sensory issues associated with ASD, for example, olfactory and tactile sensitivity, and sensitivity to bright light and the sound of machinery. It is also important that each person conducting the programme is aware of the time children with an ASD take to process and respond to social/ emotional information, and that such children are very sensitive to emotional atmosphere and attitude, especially criticism and negativity.

Conducting the sessions

Working as part of a group, there will need to be agreed ground rules on potential issues such as taking turns to speak, keeping to the point, and being courteous and friendly. Encourage your child to follow these rules.

During the first session of a group programme you will be asked to briefly introduce your son or daughter by way of age and personality characteristics, and to state your most important goal for the group. The sharing of problems/goals in this way can be a quick way to assist you and other parents to feel less alone, as you quickly discover that your problems are not unique. During the first or second session, a suggestion may be made to exchange email addresses with other parents for communication beyond the group.

The format of subsequent sessions essentially follows the sessions described in Part 3, sharing both the information given out to the children and unique information about each child during the group. The last five minutes of each session will be dedicated to sharing the project for the week and encouraging you to assist your child to complete their project.

We have found that during group sessions, a child may show remarkable moments of insight or clarity of expression. We call these 'Words of Wisdom'. There may also be moments of humour. During each group session, one of the adults presenting the course should record the key points discovered by the participants, along with any 'Words of Wisdom' or humorous comments. Print these and distribute them to the participants at the start of the next session.

Time with other parents or your own family members after each group session

At the end of each group session, there should be time with the parents of the other participants, usually 30 minutes. The aim is to exchange information regarding your children's responses and abilities during the activities, and to seek information on particular issues that could be addressed in a subsequent session. You will be encouraged to respond positively and appropriately to your child's new abilities and understanding of affection and apply the strategies discovered during the programme in real-life situations. Group discussion with parents may encourage solutions to any problems expressing affection experienced by other family members.

6

Activities for each session

Below we summarize the component activities for each session. Over the next chapters we then describe the sessions in more detail.

Session 1: Introduction to the programme – Exploring feelings of affection

Initial assessment through stories.

1. The activities and experiences that you like.

2. People whom you like or love.

3. How do those people express that they like you or love you?

4. How we feel, think and behave when someone likes or loves us.

5. What would life be like without being liked or loved?

6. List some of the things that are not so nice about being liked or loved.

7. Project: Collect pictures of people expressing affection.

8. Project: Family affection.

9. Project: Social Story™.

Session 2: Beginning to recognize and express affection

Review of Session 1.

1. A Social Story™ about how liking or loving someone can affect your feelings, thoughts and abilities.

2. Using the like and love thermometer to explore pictures of liking and loving.

3. What can you say and do to show that you like someone?

4. What can you say and do to show that you love someone?

5. Project: Use the ideas at home to express liking or loving a member of the family.

Session 3: Giving and receiving compliments

Review of Session 2.

1. Review the project from Session 2.

2. Why do we give compliments?

3. Compliments for specific people.

4. Types of compliment.

5. How often should you give someone a compliment?

6. How do you reply to a compliment?

7. Practise giving and receiving compliments.

8. Could a compliment be embarrassing?

9. Project: Create a compliment diary.

Session 4: The reasons we express like or love through affectionate words and gestures

Review of Session 3.

1. Review the compliment diary project from Session 3.

2. Why do we give affection?

3. What would happen if nobody showed you that they liked or loved you?

4. What would happen if you stopped showing your friends that you liked them?

5. If you did not get enough affection, how could you make yourself feel better?

6. How do you feel when…?

7. Project: Complete a diary of receiving and giving affection.

Session 5: Developing our skills at expressing affection

Review of Session 4.

1. Review the diary of giving and receiving affection from Session 4.

2. Different types of affection in different situations.

3. How can you tell if someone needs affection?

4. How can you tell if you have given *too much* affection?

5. How can you tell if you have given *not enough* affection?

6. What are the three most important things you have learned about affection?

7.   Complete the post-programme assessments.

8.   Express affection to someone in the group with a compliment or gesture such as a hug.

9.   Receive your certificate of knowledge.

7

Overviews of the sessions

Session 1: Introduction to the programme – Exploring feelings of affection

Initial assessment through stories

Prior to the first session you will need to complete the three affection questionnaires (from the Appendix) and your child should complete the other affection assessment measures (the three stories from Session 1 in Part 3). The information you will obtain through doing these assessments is invaluable for determining specific issues to be addressed during the programme.

Take time to review the assessments before embarking on the programme, and if possible discuss your analysis with a co-parent or someone else who knows your child well, or works with your child on a regular basis (e.g. a teacher). It will make the programme more effective if you involve other adults who are familiar with your child in your goals and projects throughout.

For this first session, you will need to distribute large sheets of paper for your child to draw thermometers, and small 'Post Its' to record specific activities, experiences or names.

If a group format is used, the session will start with an introduction of presenters and participants. Ground rules will be established and agreed, for example 'Take turns speaking', 'Be supportive of each other', 'Try to keep to the topic'.

1. The activities and experiences that you like

Ask your child to identify up to ten activities or experiences that he or she likes and to measure the degree of enjoyment on a scale of 0 to 100. Introduce the concept of a thermometer which measures the degree of feeling. Explore with your child how the same experience can be rated very similarly or very differently by different people. If your child's special interest is one of the activities or experiences, use this opportunity to explore the range of positive feelings associated with the interest.

2. People whom you like or love

This is a similar activity, but this time ask your child to identify ten people whom he or she likes or loves. These people can be family members, friends or real-life or fictional heroes. On the thermometer, 0 to 50 measures the depth of liking someone, while 51 to 100 measures the depth of love. Discuss with your child differences in the degree of liking and loving specific people and why. Try to ensure that your child's ten people illustrate different levels on the thermometer. Your child may need guidance to recognize that liking and loving is not a question of 'either/or'. Your child may wish to include a pet in the list. Use this to explore the degree of affection associated with a pet in comparison with a person.

3. How do those people express that they like you or love you?

For typical children this can be an easy activity, but a child with an ASD may have difficulty spontaneously identifying the ways people show how much he or she is liked or loved. Use examples from both family members and friends to explore the different ways of expressing affection in a friendship compared with a family. At first allow your child to make suggestions. Then make your own suggestions to see whether your child actually does or could recognize a wider range of expressions. Discuss this with other family members to explore which expressions have not been perceived or recorded by your child. Children with an ASD often prioritize and notice practical expressions of affection, such as buying a present or playing a game of their choice, yet fail to recognize words or gestures of affection, such as a hug, or being told that the family member loves them. Think of any particular words for affection that are commonly used within your family.

4. How we feel, think and behave when someone likes or loves us

This activity explores how affection can positively affect feelings, thinking and abilities. Information from this and activity 5 will be used to create a Social Story™ for the next session. (In a group format, this activity will take the form of a discussion involving all group members.) Explore important aspects of affection, such as how affection can help your child relax when anxious; re-energize, build confidence and infuse optimism when he or she is sad; and act as a quick, easy and cheap emotional restorative for friends and family members.

5. What would life be like without being liked or loved?

Discuss with your child how a lack of affection could lead to the opposite of the thoughts and feelings described in activity number 4 – for example, feeling anxious, lacking energy, having low confidence, and feeling pessimistic and sad.

6. List some of the things that are not so nice about being liked or loved

Explore with your child some of the not-so-nice aspects of being liked or loved. These might include being vulnerable to disappointment, feeling sad when someone is not there, and the need for solitude if a friend expects to be with you more than is comfortable, or expects you to be part of a larger group. Discuss concerns about sensory sensitivity, worrying about someone, and grief, should a relative (such as a grandparent) die.

7. Project: Collect pictures of people expressing affection

Ask your child to collect pictures of people expressing affection. These pictures will be used in an activity in Session 2. Look for pictures in magazines for women and families, for adolescents, gossip magazines or internet clip art. Include copies of family photographs where family members are expressing affection.

8. Project: Family affection

Ask your child to identify situations where affection is expected, but which he or she finds difficult. Although you will probably want to focus on your close family members, you can also include your wider family circle and other significant people in your child's life such as a teacher, and friends or classmates. The information will be used in a subsequent activity.

9. Project: Social Story™

Between sessions, write a Social Story™ using material from activities 4 and 5 in Session 1.

Social Stories™ were originally developed by Carol Gray (see Recommended Resources). A Social Story™ describes a situation, skill or concept in terms of relevant social cues, perspectives and common responses in a specifically defined style and format. The intention is to share accurate social and emotional information in a reassuring and informative manner that is easily understood by the child with Asperger's syndrome. Carol Gray has developed a Social Story™ formula such that the text describes more than directs. More information is available from www.thegraycenter.org.

> If running the program in a group format with other parents, it is useful to meet immediately after Session 1 to discuss what happened, how each child responded to the material and how best to manage the different personalities and dynamics that may be occurring in the group. Discuss how to support each other to ensure the project is completed each week. The project is important because it provides valuable information and the opportunity to improve the communication of affection in real situations.

Session 2: Beginning to recognize and express affection

Begin this session with a revision of the key points and words of wisdom from the last session. Use a quick quiz to enable your child to recall someone who is liked or loved and how much, using the scale or thermometer from 0 to 100.

1. A Social Story™ about how liking or loving someone can affect your feelings, thoughts and abilities

Read aloud the Social Story™ or stories using your child's suggestions about how liking or loving someone can affect feelings, thoughts and behaviour.

2. Using the like and love thermometer to explore pictures of liking and loving

The first part of the project was to collect pictures or photographs that illustrate different levels of liking or loving someone. Draw a thermometer on a very large piece of paper on the floor. Ask your child to place each of his or her pictures at the appropriate point on the thermometer. You may need to offer guidance and discuss any unusual rating of the degree of affection.

Part of this activity can be to learn the words and facial expressions that describe different levels of affection, from 'concerned' to 'loving'. *The Cognitive Affective Training kit* or *CAT-kit* (see Recommended Resources) can be used as an additional resource to improve your child's vocabulary to describe different levels of affection.

3. What can you say and do to show that you like someone?

Working with your child, one of you creates a list of actions or statements that you can do or say to show that you like someone. The other one also rates, from 1 to 50, the degree of liking that each action or statement indicates. When the list has at least five examples, reverse roles. (If your child prefers not to write, you may need to be the scribe for both roles.)

When the lists are completed, discuss the actions and statements, providing your child with an opportunity to learn new expressions of liking someone.

An additional activity can be to explore how animals, and especially pets, express liking someone.

4. What can you say and do to show that you love someone?

Follow the same format as in the previous activity, this time for love, with a rating from 51 to 100.

Discuss with your child the different degree of affection expressed by specific actions, and variations in the quality, intensity and duration of an action. For example, your child may have a limited 'vocabulary' of hugs – one size fits all. Use role-play activities to discover different types of hug, perhaps with a numerical value from 1 to 10 that reflects the degree of affection being expressed and exchanged. Also discuss different types of kiss, from greeting a distant family member to expressing love to a parent. Use a silhouette of a body to discuss where on the body is an appropriate place to kiss according to your own cultural and family conventions.

Feedback from Session 1 project for a group format

In turn, the participants share with the group their findings from the Session 1 project. They each describe a situation where affection is anticipated with a particular family member. Together, they make suggestions as to when affection should be expressed in the particular situation described, and to what degree. The participants record these suggestions on their handouts.

5. Project: Use the ideas at home to express liking or loving a member of the family

The project between Sessions 2 and 3 is for your child to actually express affection for the nominated family member, using the ideas discussed in Session 2, and to discuss at the next session what he or she did or said, what was the reaction of the family member and how that family member felt. Extend this, if appropriate, to include expressions of affection for significant adults or friends and classmates.

Session 3: Giving and receiving compliments

Start the third session with a reminder of what happened in the previous session. Discuss key points and words of wisdom.

1. Review the project from Session 2

First, discuss the project. Explore with your child situations within the family (or friendship) where there is an expectation of affection. Ask your child to provide feedback on who was the recipient, the type of affection, the response of the other person, and how he or she felt when expressing affection. Emphasize the positive consequences for both the person receiving and the person giving affection.

The main theme for Session 3 is giving and receiving compliments.

2. Why do we give compliments?

This activity explores the thoughts and feelings that your child is expressing when he or she gives a family member or friend a compliment. Compliments can be divided into five categories of thoughts or feelings:

- admiration

- reassurance

- friendship

- encouragement

- liking or loving someone.

3. Compliments for specific people

In the first activity, ask your child to suggest a compliment for a friend for each of the five categories of thoughts or feelings described above. Then ask your child to create a compliment for specific family members for four of the same five categories (in this instance, 'friendship' is not needed).

4. Types of compliment

Your child may need guidance regarding what qualities in a person can be appropriately acknowledged by a compliment. This activity is designed to explore the different types of compliment that can be expressed about someone's abilities, appearance and personality. Ask your child to create a compliment for a friend or family member based on these attributes.

5. How often should you give someone a compliment?

As described in the introduction to this programme, children, and often adults, with an ASD may not express affection as frequently as would be expected and appreciated by a friend or family member. Giving someone a compliment can be an expression of affection. Explain to your child that compliments should not be a rare expression of liking or loving someone and should probably be expressed to a friend or family member on a more frequent basis.

6. How do you reply to a compliment?

This activity is designed to provide guidance and discussion on how to respond to a compliment. The two main anticipated responses are to express appreciation and agreement. Ask your child to create examples of how to express appreciation and agreement.

7. Practise giving and receiving compliments

Together with your child, practise giving and responding to compliments, and explore and share the feelings of the person giving and the person receiving the compliment. This can be a very enjoyable activity.

8. Could a compliment be embarrassing?

Children with an ASD may not be as aware as typical peers of social conventions when giving a compliment, or as able to perceive and appreciate that the compliment they are giving may be true but could be embarrassing for the recipient. This activity explores the types of compliment that could be embarrassing for a classmate, friend or family member. Discuss with your child why some compliments could be perceived as embarrassing, and how to recognize the signals. This activity is particularly important for teenagers seeking a relationship beyond friendship. Role plays and the use of specific resources, such as the interactive DVD *Mind Reading: The Interactive Guide to Emotions* (see Recommended Resources) can help your child identify the verbal and non-verbal signs of embarrassment.

9. Project: Create a compliment diary

The project between sessions is for your child to keep a diary of compliments that he or she receives and gives each day.

Session 4: The reasons we express like or love through affectionate words and gestures

Session 4 begins in the usual way, reviewing the key points and words of wisdom from Session 3.

1. Review the compliment diary project from Session 3

Follow with a brief review of compliments, with discussion of the feelings of the person giving and receiving the compliment, and any subsequent effects on the friendship or relationship.

2. Why do we give affection?

Now that the expression of affection has been explored over three sessions, ask your child to suggest reasons why people give each other affection. Some of the answers may already have been generated early in Session 1, but at this stage there will be more reasons identified and appreciated. Compare the two lists to see what has been learned and appreciated.

3. What would happen if nobody showed you that they liked or loved you?

This activity explores how your child would feel if he or she did not experience demonstrations of being liked or loved.

Use these responses to lead into the next activity and to illustrate how a friend or relative would feel if expressions of affection were not made by your child to that person.

4. What would happen if you stopped showing your friends that you liked them?

Explore further the theme of feeling bereft of affection, primarily for a friend, although the discussion can progress to how a family member would feel. The activity also includes strategies to repair the feelings of a friend (or family member) associated with not experiencing expressions of affection.

5. If you did not get enough affection, how could you make yourself feel better?

This activity is helpful for children who may feel that they do not experience enough affection. You or your co-parent may also have a problem expressing affection at times so you could take part in this activity and use it as an opportunity to share and explore strategies to cope, cheer yourself up and achieve compensatory affection from someone else, or a pet.

> This activity can be an important point of discussion when you meet other children's parents if doing the programme as a group, or when you discuss the session with your co-parent and other family members.

6. How do you feel when...?

Use the questionnaire to explore the depth of enjoyment or discomfort your child experiences in response to specific expressions of affection, for example when Mum or Dad say 'I love you'.

7. Project: Complete a diary of receiving and giving affection

You and your child complete a diary for six very specific expressions of affection. The intention is to actively encourage expressing each type of affection at least twice a day, and to record an example of these expressions of affection. Actively support your child to complete the log book each day.

Session 5: Developing our skills at expressing affection

Begin with a brief review of the key points and words of wisdom from Session 4. Session 5 starts with recalling the feelings associated with experiencing affection. Discuss the consequences for your child if he or she did not express affection to a friend or family member.

1. Review the diary of receiving and giving affection from Session 4

Review, share and discuss the information and experiences recorded in the diary of receiving and giving affection.

2. Different types of affection in different situations

In this activity your child plays a game to match specific types of affection to a particular situation. There are appropriate matches, but you can also have some fun making inappropriate matches, and exploring why they are inappropriate – for example, saying to the postman, 'I love you', or giving your mum a handshake when she is crying.

3. How can you tell if someone needs affection?

This activity can be very difficult for children with an ASD, especially with regard to identifying subtle signals. Additional activities and resources could be used; for example, you could role play (and replay on video) someone who is expressing subtle signs of distress and ask your child which non-verbal cues indicated a need for affection and what would be an appropriate response if that person was a friend or family member. Short video clips and audio recordings from *Mind Reading: The Interactive Guide to Emotions* (see Recommended Resources) can be used to supplement and extend the activity if needed.

In a group format, children can work in pairs and use role play to practise expressing and recognizing the subtle signals of someone needing affection.

4. How can you tell if you have given too much affection?

This is a similar activity and requires your child to read the non-verbal signs of someone feeling uncomfortable, embarrassed or annoyed when he or she is the recipient of too much affection. Role playing and video recording can be used to illustrate the signs.

5. How can you tell if you have given not enough affection?

Use this activity to explore subtle non-verbal communication signals. Role play and additional resources may also be used.

6. What are the three most important things you have learned about affection?

This is an opportunity to share important new knowledge.

7. Complete the post-programme assessments

Use these assessments to record changes in abilities and knowledge, also including your child's responses to the three stories used in the assessment in the first session: 'A Walk in the Forest', 'Returning Home from School' and 'A Friend Feeling Sad' (see Session 1 in Part 3). Compare the number and type of responses for your child between the start and end of the programme. This can confirm an increase in the understanding of the value of affection. You will also need to complete the three affection questionnaires at the end of the programme. Ask your child which aspects of the programme he or she found especially enjoyable, informative or difficult, and how the programme could be improved.

8. Express affection to someone in the group with a compliment or gesture such as a hug
This is a closing activity when the programme is in a group format to express appreciation and affection for all participants and presenters.

9. Receive your certificate of knowledge!
A certificate of knowledge, signed by you (or by presenters in a group format), is awarded to the child.

Part 3

Sessions

Readers have permission to photocopy all worksheets marked with a ✓ for personal use with this programme. They are also available to download from www.jkp.com/catalogue/book/9781849054362/resources.

Session 1

Introduction to the programme

Exploring feelings of affection

✓

Initial assessment through stories

Read the 'A Walk in the Forest', 'Returning Home from School' and 'A Friend Feeling Sad' stories below and complete the related activities.

A WALK IN THE FOREST

Imagine it is early morning and you are walking along a path in a forest. As you come to the middle of the forest, you notice that several trees have fallen to the ground. You are curious, as you know that there have been no high winds recently that would explain why the trees have come down. As you climb over the tree trunks, you see that in the middle of the fallen trees there is what looks like a small space ship.

As you carefully approach it, there is a strange noise and an opening appears at the front of the space ship. Out of the opening comes a glowing object, about the size and shape of a tennis ball. The glowing shape hovers just above you, and then slowly descends to become level with your eyes. Suddenly it disappears and there in front of you is someone who looks exactly like you.

✓

The person who looks exactly the same as you starts to speak, with a voice the same as yours. This duplicate 'you' explains that it is an alien that has crashed on planet earth while observing humans. It explains that the spaceship will be repaired in a few hours, but before leaving, the alien has a very important question to ask you about humans.

The alien has observed that humans seem to need to communicate that they like or love one another, and that they do this by saying nice things to each other and touching one another. It has observed that this behaviour seems to happen particularly between friends and family members. The alien is curious as to why humans do this.

Can you explain to the alien why humans are affectionate with each other?

. . . .

. . . .

. . . .

. . . .

The alien now understands and gives you a special present. What present could the alien give you?

. . . .

. . . .

. . . .

. . . .

✓

RETURNING HOME FROM SCHOOL

Imagine you have just returned home from school. You walk into the kitchen to let your mother know that you are home. You see that she is sitting at the kitchen table with her back to you. As you say 'Hi', she turns round and you notice that she is crying.

What would you do or say first?

. . . .

. . . .

. . . .

. . . .

What could you do or say to make her feel better?

. . . .

. . . .

. . . .

. . . .

A FRIEND FEELING SAD

Imagine you have arrived at school, just before your friend. As your friend enters the school grounds, you notice your friend looks very sad. Your friend explains that early that morning, his or her dog escaped from home, ran across a road, was hit by a car, and died.

What could you do or say to make your friend feel better?

. . . .

. . . .

. . . .

. . . .

1. The activities and experiences that you like

We all have activities and experiences that we like. Think of up to ten activities or experiences you like and write them in the spaces below.

Activity or experience	How much you enjoy the activity or experience

Some activities and experiences we like very much, others just a little.

Now imagine a scale from 1 to 100.

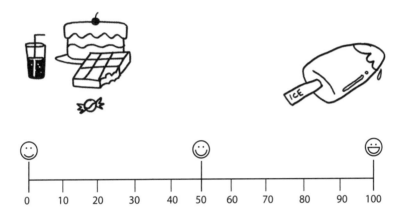

1–10 represents something we like just a little bit.

90–100 represents something we really like a lot.

Next to each activity or experience write the number from 0 to 100 for how much you like each one. You can choose any number in between, depending on how much you like the activity. Think carefully before you choose the number.

The person who is helping you will then write down each activity or experience on a yellow 'Post It', and draw a feeling thermometer that measures how strong the feeling is from 0 to 100. You can then stick each 'Post It' at the position on the thermometer that measures how much you like that activity or experience.

If you are in a group, look at the thermometer of each of the children in the group and see if you share any of the same activities, experiences and intensity of feeling.

2. People whom you like or love

Make a list of ten people whom you like or love and write each name in the spaces under the word 'Person'. The person can be someone from your family or a hero from a film, television programme or book.

Person	How much you like that person

✓

Some people we know we like or love very much, other people we like or love just a little.

Imagine a scale from 1 to 100.

1–10 represents someone we like just a little bit.

90–100 represents someone we love a lot.

Next to each activity or experience write the number from 0 to 100 for how much you like or love each person.

You can choose any number in between, depending on how much you like or love the person.

Liking someone may be measured from 0 to 50, and loving someone from 50 to 100.

Think carefully before you choose the number.

The person who is helping you will write down the name of each person on a yellow 'Post It' and draw another feeling thermometer that measures how strong the feeling of liking or loving that person is from 0 to 100. You can then stick each 'Post It' at the position on the thermometer that measures how much you like or love that person.

3. How do those people express that they like you or love you?

List all the ways you can think of that people show you how much they like you or love you.

. . . .

. . . .

. . . .

. . . .

. . . .

. . . .

. . . .

. . . .

. . . .

4. How we feel, think and behave when someone likes or loves us

List some of the good things about being liked or loved.

How does being liked or loved affect our feelings, thoughts and abilities?

For example:

When someone likes or loves me, I feel…

. . . .

. . . .

. . . .

. . . .

When someone likes or loves me, I think...

. . . .

. . . .

. . . .

. . . .

When someone likes or loves me, I am able to...

. . . .

. . . .

. . . .

. . . .

✓

5. What would life be like without being liked or loved?

· ·

· ·

· ·

· ·

· ·

· ·

· ·

· ·

6. List some of the things that are not so nice about being liked or loved

. . . .

. . . .

. . . .

. . . .

. . . .

. . . .

. . . .

. . . .

7. Project: Collect pictures of expressing affection

Find, cut out and save pictures or drawings of people your age expressing that they like or love someone. You might find some pictures in magazines, in clip art on your computer, or on the internet. You will need to collect about 10 to 20 pictures. Keep the pictures in a large envelope and bring the envelope and pictures with you to the next session.

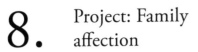

8. Project: Family affection

Sometimes you might find it difficult to express your feelings of love towards your family.

Get your family to think of (and write down) some of those situations where they would expect you to express that you like them or love them, but that you find difficult.

....

....

....

....

....

....

....

✓

9. Project : Social Story™

Ask your family to help you to write a Social Story™ about how liking or loving someone can affect your feelings, thoughts and abilities, using some of the ideas from today's session.

....

....

....

....

....

....

....

....

....

Session 2

Beginning to recognize and express affection

Review of Session 1

Last time we explored some interesting topics: activities and experiences that you like; people who you like; and how we express affection. Let's do a quick quiz to see how much you can remember.

Name one person who you like. How much do you like them (1–50)?

. . . .

Name one person who you love. How much do you love them (50–100)?

. . . .

How does that person express their love for you?

. . . .

. . . .

How does that make you feel?

. . . .

. . . .

What else did you learn from the last session?

. . . .

. . . .

✓

1. A Social Story™ about how liking or loving someone can affect your feelings, thoughts and abilities

Include the Social Story™ you have been given here.

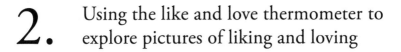

2. Using the like and love thermometer to explore pictures of liking and loving

Now you will need the envelope with all the pictures of affection that you collected over the past week.

On the wall there is a 'thermometer' marked from 0 to 100.

1–10 represents 'I like the person a little bit.'

Under 50 shows 'I like the person.'

Over 50 shows 'I love the person.'

90–100 represents 'I love the person a lot.'

For each of the pictures that you have collected think about how much loving or liking is being expressed in the picture. Place the picture on the thermometer where you think it should go.

3. What can you say and do to show that you like someone?

Your parent or the person who is helping you will write down all things you can say and do to show that you like someone. Use the scale from 1 to 50 to say how much liking is expressed by each action or statement.

Things to say and do to show that you like the person	How much liking does this show? (1–50)

4. What can you say and do to show that you love someone?

Your parent or the person who is helping you will write down all the things you can say and do to show that you love someone. Use the scale from 50 to 100 to say how is expressed by each action or statement.

Things to say and do to show that you love the person	How much loving does this show? (50–100)

5. Project: Use the ideas at home to express liking or loving a member of the family

Sometimes you might find it difficult to express your feelings of love towards your family.

Last week your family thought of (and wrote down) a situation where they would expect you to express that you like them or love them, but that you find difficult.

What was that situation?

. . . .

. . . .

. . . .

Your project is to use some of the ideas from today's session to express liking or loving to a member of your family this week.

When will you express affection?

. . . .

. . . .

What type of affection will you express?

. . . .

. . . .

Session 3

Giving and receiving compliments

Review of Session 2

We are really exploring affection deeply now.

Last time we placed our liking and loving pictures on the feeling thermometer.

We then wrote down things you can do or say to show that you like or love someone and how much liking or loving is expressed for each action or statement.

1. Review the project from Session 2

Your family thought of (and wrote down) a situation where someone would expect you to express that you like them or love them, but that you find difficult.

Who was the person?

. . . .

What was that situation?

. . . .

. . . .

Your project was to express liking or loving a member of your family in the last week, using some of the ideas you discovered in Session 2.

When did you express affection?

. . . .

. . . .

What type of affection did you express?

. . . .

. . . .

What did that person say and how did that person feel when you expressed your affection?

. . . .

. . . .

. . . .

. . . .

How did you feel when you expressed affection?

. . . .

. . . .

. . . .

. . . .

2. Why do we give compliments?

A compliment is when we say something nice about someone.

Compliments express feelings or thoughts of:

- admiration

- reassurance

- friendship

- encouragement

- liking or loving someone.

When we give a compliment to someone it means we:

. . . .

. . . .

. . . .

. . . .

✓

3. Compliments for specific people

Write a compliment for a friend that expresses:

admiration

. . . .

. . . .

. . . .

reassurance

. . . .

. . . .

. . . .

friendship

. . . .

. . . .

. . . .

encouragement

. . . .

. . . .

. . . .

liking that person

. . . .

. . . .

. . . .

Write a compliment for your brother or sister (if you have one) that expresses:

admiration

. . . .

. . . .

. . . .

reassurance

. . . .

. . . .

. . . .

encouragement

. . . .

. . . .

. . . .

loving that person

. . . .

. . . .

. . . .

✓

Write a compliment for your mother or father that expresses:

admiration

. . . .

. . . .

. . . .

reassurance

. . . .

. . . .

. . . .

encouragement

. . . .

. . . .

. . . .

loving that person

. . . .

. . . .

. . . .

4. Types of compliment

A compliment can be about a person's:

- abilities

- appearance

- personality.

Write a compliment that you could give your friend about his or her:

abilities

. . . .

. . . .

. . . .

appearance

. . . .

. . . .

. . . .

personality

. . . .

. . . .

. . . .

Write a compliment that you could give your father or mother about his or her:

abilities

. . . .

. . . .

. . . .

✓

appearance

. . . .

. . . .

. . . .

personality

. . . .

. . . .

. . . .

5. How often should you give someone a compliment?

Suggest how many times a day or week you should give a compliment to a:

	Times a day	Times a week
classmate		
friend		
brother or sister		
mother or father		

6. How do you reply to a compliment?

When you hear a compliment about you, you can express:

- appreciation

- agreement.

Think of some examples of:

appreciation

. . . .

. . . .

. . . .

✓

agreement

. . . .

. . . .

. . . .

7. Practise giving and receiving compliments

Think of a compliment you could give someone for his or her abilities, appearance or personality.

Actually say that compliment to the person.

How did that person feel when you said the compliment?

. . . .

. . . .

. . . .

How did *you* feel when they expressed their appreciation?

. . . .

. . . .

. . . .

8. Could a compliment be embarrassing?

Sometimes a compliment could be embarrassing to the person who hears it. Can you think of a compliment that could be embarrassing, and why, if it was to a...

classmate

. . . .

. . . .

. . . .

friend

. . . .

. . . .

. . . .

brother or sister

. . . .

. . . .

. . . .

mother or father

. . . .

. . . .

. . . .

9. Project: Create a compliment diary

Keep a diary of compliments that you receive and give each day.

Session 4

The reasons we express like or love through affectionate words and gestures

✓

Review of Session 3

Last time we learned about giving and receiving compliments. Let's see how much you can remember.

Can you think of a compliment for a friend?

. . . .

. . . .

. . . .

✓

Can you think of a compliment for your mum or dad?

. . . .

. . . .

. . . .

What else did you learn from the last session?

. . . .

. . . .

. . . .

✓

1. Review the compliment diary project from Session 3

Over the past week, you kept a diary of compliments that you received and gave each day.

What compliments did you receive?

. . . .

. . . .

. . . .

. . . .

Who were the compliments from?

. . . .

. . . .

How did you feel when you received the compliments?

. . . .

. . . .

. . . .

. . . .

What compliments did you give?

. . . .

. . . .

. . . .

. . . .

Who did you give them to?

. . . .

. . . .

. . . .

. . . .

How did you feel when you gave these compliments?

. . . .

. . . .

. . . .

. . . .

2. Why do we give affection?

Sometimes the reason a person gives affection can be puzzling.

Why do you think people give each other affection? See how many reasons you can think of, then share them with the group.

. . . .

. . . .

. . . .

. . . .

. . . .

. . . .

. . . .

3. What would happen if nobody showed you that they liked or loved you?

Draw a picture of your face here…

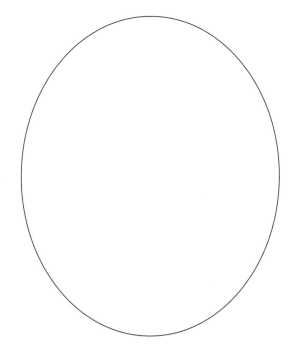

How would you feel?

. . . .

. . . .

. . . .

✓

What would you say?

. . . .

. . . .

. . . .

What would you do?

. . . .

. . . .

. . . .

4.

What would happen if you stopped showing your friends that you liked them?

Draw a picture of your friend's face here…

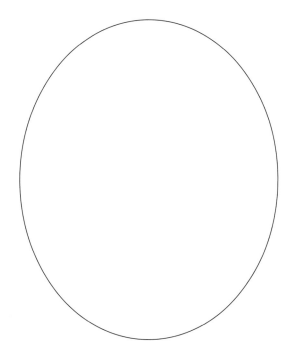

How would he or she feel?

. . . .

. . . .

. . . .

✓

What could you say to help him or her feel better?

. . . .

. . . .

. . . .

What could you do to help him or her feel better?

. . . .

. . . .

. . . .

5. If you did not get enough affection, how could you make yourself feel better?

Things I could do to cheer myself up:

. . . .

. . . .

. . . .

. . . .

. . . .

. . . .

✓

6. How do you feel when...?

Circle the number that measures how you feel when...

(a) Your mum gives you a kiss on the cheek

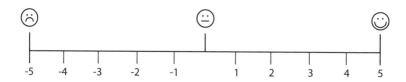

(b) A friend puts his or her arm around your shoulders

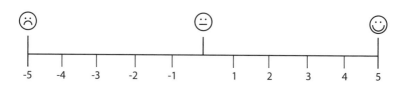

(c) Your mum or dad says, 'I love you'

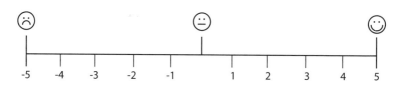

(d) A friend says, 'Well done'

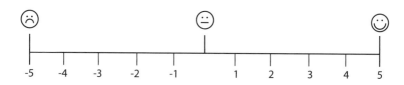

(e) Your dad gives you a quick hug

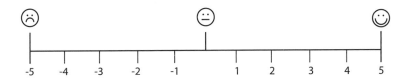

(f) Your mum says you have nice eyes

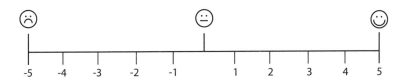

(g) Your mum wants to hold your hand

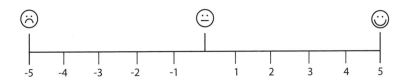

(h) A friend says, 'You are a great friend'

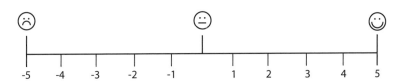

✓

7. Project: Complete a diary of receiving and giving affection

We have a diary for you and your parent or carer to complete over the next week that provides a record of when you expressed affection and some exapes of the type of affection.

Your name: _____

Please place a ✔ in the box when you have expressed each type of affection.

See if you can express each type of affection at least twice a day.

Types of affection	Wednesday	Thursday	Friday	Saturday	Sunday	Monday	Tuesday
Listen	☐ ☐ ☐	☐ ☐ ☐	☐ ☐ ☐	☐ ☐ ☐	☐ ☐ ☐	☐ ☐ ☐	☐ ☐ ☐
Spend fun time with the person	☐ ☐ ☐	☐ ☐ ☐	☐ ☐ ☐	☐ ☐ ☐	☐ ☐ ☐	☐ ☐ ☐	☐ ☐ ☐
Do something helpful for the person	☐ ☐ ☐	☐ ☐ ☐	☐ ☐ ☐	☐ ☐ ☐	☐ ☐ ☐	☐ ☐ ☐	☐ ☐ ☐
Say 'I love you'	☐ ☐ ☐	☐ ☐ ☐	☐ ☐ ☐	☐ ☐ ☐	☐ ☐ ☐	☐ ☐ ☐	☐ ☐ ☐
Kiss or hug the person	☐ ☐ ☐	☐ ☐ ☐	☐ ☐ ☐	☐ ☐ ☐	☐ ☐ ☐	☐ ☐ ☐	☐ ☐ ☐
Give the person a compliment	☐ ☐ ☐	☐ ☐ ☐	☐ ☐ ☐	☐ ☐ ☐	☐ ☐ ☐	☐ ☐ ☐	☐ ☐ ☐

Your name: _____

In the spaces provided, briefly record the situations in which you received each of the different types of affection, and who showed them to you.

Types of affection	Wednesday	Thursday	Friday	Saturday	Sunday	Monday	Tuesday
Listen							
Spend fun time with the person							
Do something helpful for the person							
Say 'I love you'							
Kiss or hug the person							
Give the person a compliment							

Session 5

Developing our skills at expressing affection

Review of Session 4

Last time we explored reasons why we express feelings of like or love by words and gestures of affection. Can you remember some of the feelings you have when someone is affectionate to you?

. . . .

. . . .

. . . .

What could happen if you did not show affection to a friend or someone in your family?

. . . .

. . . .

. . . .

✓

1. Review the diary of receiving and giving affection from Session 4

Review, share and discuss the information and experiences recorded in your diary of receiving and giving affection.

Consider these questions:

Did you enjoy expressing affection?

. . . .

Which types? To whom?

. . . .

. . . .

Did you enjoy receiving affection?

. . . .

Which types? By whom?

. . . .

. . . .

Did you express too much or too little affection?

. . . .

How did you know?

. . . .

. . . .

Did you receive enough affection?

. . . .

Are there any situations in which you do not like to give or receive affection? What are they?

. . . .

. . . .

2. Different types of affection in different situations

The matching game

On the following page there is a list of situations and a list of different types of affection. See if you can match the best type of affection for the situation by drawing a line between the situation and the type of affection.

Situation	Type of affection
Your dad or carer is trying to talk to someone on the phone and doing the washing-up at the same time.	Pat on the head
Your mum or carer smiles at you.	Hand shake
It is bedtime and time to say 'good night' to your parent or carer.	Close, long hug
It is time to go to school and time to say 'goodbye' to your parent or carer.	Quick kiss on the cheek
Your friend hits a difficult-to-hit ball in a tennis game.	Hold hands
Your parent or carer says, 'I love you.'	Kiss on the lips
A stranger says, 'Hello' and holds out their hand.	Saying, 'You are my best friend'
The postman comes to your house.	Saying, 'I love you'
Your parent or carer is crying.	Arm around the shoulders
Your friend has fallen off his or her bike and has hurt himself.	Quick hug
Your aunt has come to visit and it is time to say 'Hello' to her.	Saying, 'You have nice eyes'
You see someone you do not know.	Saying, 'Well done!'
Your mum or carer cooks you your favourite meal.	Pat on the back
Your friend gives you a pat on the back.	Saying, 'Thank you'
Your friend gives you a nice present.	Saying, 'I like the way you did that'

✓

3. How can you tell if someone needs affection?

What are the signs that someone needs affection? Think of the person's facial expression, body language, words and tone of voice, the situation and what you know about that person. Think of the signs you would notice in different situations.

Facial expression

. . . .

. . . .

. . . .

Body language

. . . .

. . . .

. . . .

Words

. . . .

. . . .

. . . .

Tone of voice

. . . .

. . . .

. . . .

✓

The situation

. . . .

. . . .

. . . .

What you know about the person

. . . .

. . . .

. . . .

See if you can you have a go expressing those signs yourself and noticing them in the facial expression, body language and tone of voice of the person you are working with.

4. How can you tell if you have given *too much* affection?

What are the signs in someone's facial expression, body language and words?

Facial expression

. . . .

. . . .

. . . .

Body language

. . . .

. . . .

. . . .

✓

Words

. . . .

. . . .

. . . .

How will that person feel?

. . . .

. . . .

. . . .

5. How can you tell if you have given *not enough* affection?

What are the signs in someone's facial expression, body language and words?

Facial expression

. . . .

. . . .

. . . .

Body language

. . . .

. . . .

. . . .

Words

. . . .

. . . .

. . . .

How will that person feel?

. . . .

. . . .

. . . .

6. What are the three most important things you have learned about affection?

1.

. . . .

. . . .

2.

. . . .

. . . .

3.

. . . .

. . . .

✓

7. Complete the post-programme assessments

Complete the 'A Walk in the Forest', 'Returning Home from School' and 'A Friend Feeling Sad' activities from Session 1 again.

A WALK IN THE FOREST

Imagine it is early morning and you are walking along a path in a forest. As you come to the middle of the forest, you notice that several trees have fallen to the ground. You are curious, as you know that there have been no high winds recently that would explain why the trees have come down. As you climb over the tree trunks, you see that in the middle of the fallen trees there is what looks like a small space ship.

As you carefully approach it, there is a strange noise and an opening appears at the front of the space ship. Out of the opening comes a glowing object, about the size and shape of a tennis ball. The glowing shape hovers just above you, and then slowly descends to become level with your eyes. Suddenly it disappears and there in front of you is someone who looks exactly like you.

✓

The person who looks exactly the same as you starts to speak, with a voice the same as yours. This duplicate 'you' explains that it is an alien that has crashed on planet earth while observing humans. It explains that the space ship will be repaired in a few hours, but before leaving, the alien has a very important question to ask you about humans.

The alien has observed that humans seem to need to communicate that they like or love one another, and that they do this by saying nice things to each other and touching one another. It has observed that this behaviour seems to happen particularly between friends and family members. The alien is curious as to why humans do this.

Can you explain to the alien why humans are affectionate with each other?

. . . .

. . . .

. . . .

. . . .

The alien now understands and gives you a special present. What present could the alien give you?

. . . .

. . . .

. . . .

. . . .

RETURNING HOME FROM SCHOOL

Imagine you have just returned home from school. You walk into the kitchen to let your mother know that you are home. You see that she is sitting at the kitchen table with her back to you. As you say 'Hi', she turns round and you notice that she is crying.

What would you do or say first?

. . . .

. . . .

. . . .

. . . .

What could you do or say to make her feel better?

. . . .

. . . .

. . . .

. . . .

✓

A FRIEND FEELING SAD

Imagine you have arrived at school, just before your friend. As your friend enters the school grounds, you notice your friend looks very sad. Your friend explains that early that morning, his or her dog escaped from home, ran across a road, was hit by a car, and died.

What could you do or say to make your friend feel better?

. . . .

. . . .

. . . .

. . . .

✓

How has your understanding of affection changed since the beginning of the programme?

. . . .

. . . .

. . . .

. . . .

8. Express affection to someone in the group with a compliment or gesture such as a hug

9. Receive your certificate of knowledge!

References

Grandin, T. and Barron, S. (2005) *Unwritten Rules of Social Relationships.* Arlington, TX: Future Horizons.

Sofronoff, K., Eloff, J., Sheffield, J. and Attwood, T. (2011) 'Increasing the understanding and demonstration of appropriate affection in children with Asperger syndrome: *A pilot trial.'* *Autism Research and Treatment*, volume 2011. doi:10.1155/2011/214317.

Sofronoff, K., Lee, J., Sheffield, J. and Attwood, T. (in press) 'The construction and evaluation of three measures of affectionate behaviour for children with Asperger's syndrome.' *Autism.*

Recommended Resources

CAT-kit by Kirsten Callesen, Annette Moller-Nielsen and Tony Attwood published in 2008 by Future Horizons, Arlington, Texas.

The New Social Story Book by Carol Gray published in 2010 by Future Horizons, Arlington, Texas.

Mind Reading: The Interactive Guide to Emotions DVD by Simon Baron-Cohen, distributed by Jessica Kingsley Publishers, London. The programme uses an interactive DVD and can be used with children from age six to adults. More information available from www.jkp.com.

Appendix

Affection Questionnaires

Adapted from Sofronoff, Lee, Sheffield and Attwood (in press).

Scoring and understanding the affection questionnaires

Important background

The questionnaire was given to 54 children (aged 5–13 years old) with Asperger's syndrome who participated in a trial of the Affection programme (Andrews, Attwood and Sofronoff, under review). Each of these children completed the questionnaire at the start and at the end of the programme. An average score was calculated each time by adding up all the children's scores and dividing by the number of children.

The Affection for Others Questionnaire (AOQ)

The AOQ is a 20-item questionnaire that examines giving and receiving verbal and physical affection, and the communication of empathy by the child, to *classmates*, *friends* and *family members*. There are four questions within each subscale, making a total of 20 questions.

There are two parts to each question. The first part asks you about the *appropriateness* of your child's affectionate gestures. Scores range from 1, 'Never appropriate', through to 7, 'Always appropriate'. The second part of the question assesses the *amount* of affection that your child displays, with responses ranging from 1, 'Not enough', to 7, 'Too much'.

To score the AOQ, add up the *appropriateness* (the first part of the question) and *amount* (the second part of the question) scores separately to give a Total Appropriateness score and a Total Amount of Affection score.

UNDERSTANDING THE TOTAL APPROPRIATENESS SCORE

In the trial of the Affection programme, the average Total Appropriateness score for a child with Asperger's syndrome (aged 5–13 years old) was 66 at the start of the programme, and 77 at the end of the programme (Andrews *et al.*, under review). The research trial indicated that most of the children improved in how appropriately they showed affection.

It may be useful for you to compare your child's Total Appropriateness score with the averages from this research trial, to determine how appropriately he or she demonstrates affection compared to other children with Asperger's syndrome. Measured before and after the Affection programme, the Total Appropriateness score will be a good indicator of how much improvement your child experiences as a result of the Affection programme.

UNDERSTANDING THE TOTAL AMOUNT OF AFFECTION SCORE

Scores of 59 and below are considered 'Low affection', scores between 59 and 100 are considered 'Adequate affection', and scores 101 and above are considered 'High affection'. A desired outcome of the Affection programme is that your child is demonstrating 'Adequate affection'.

The Affection for You Questionnaire (AYQ)

The AYQ is a 19-item questionnaire that examines giving and receiving verbal and physical affection, and the communication of empathy by the child, to a *parent.*

Similar to the AOQ, there are two parts to each question. The first part of the question measures the frequency of affection shown to you, on a scale from 1, 'Never', to 7, 'Twice a day or more'. This part of the questionnaire is a qualitative measure and no score is calculated. The second part of the question measures the amount of affection your child shows, Total Affection, on a scale from 1, 'Not enough', to 7, 'Too much'.

To calculate the Total Affection score, add up all of the scores for the second part of each question in the questionnaire.

UNDERSTANDING THE TOTAL AFFECTION SCORE

A score of 57 and below is considered 'Low affection', a score between 57 and 95 is denoted as 'Adequate affection', and a score of 96 or over is categorized as 'High affection'. As for the AOQ above, a desired outcome is that the child shows 'Adequate affection'.

The General Affection Questionnaire (GAQ)

The GAQ is a 12-item questionnaire that examines aspects of affectionate communication such as expressing inadequate or excessive affection, the importance of affection in your child's daily life, and the degree to which teaching and support regarding affection are required. To complete the questionnaire, assign a rating from 1, 'Strongly disagree', to 7, 'Strongly agree', to each of 12 statements. These statements variously assess the amount of affection the child shows, the appropriateness of that affection, the impact of the difficulties with affection your child has, and your child's knowledge of affection.

To score, simply sum all of the 12 items to give a Total Difficulty with Affection score.

UNDERSTANDING THE TOTAL DIFFICULTY WITH AFFECTION SCORE

In the trial of the Affection programme, the average score for the 54 children (aged 5–13 years old) with Asperger's syndrome was 42 (Andrews *et al.*, under review).

It may be useful to compare your own child's score to this average. The GAQ was found to be most useful in the initial assessment of children's affection difficulties, to discover where the child's difficulties lie.

The Affection for Others Questionnaire (AOQ)

The questions below are all to do with the types of affection your child (aged between 5 years and 13 years old) with autism spectrum disorder shows *others*. This means the affection that he or she shows to people outside of his or her immediate family such as: school teachers, classmates, family friends, shopkeepers and strangers. Please fill this out even if your child has very few difficulties expressing affection for others.

There are two components to each question:

1. How appropriately does your child show others that form of affection?

Consider how **appropriately** your child shows affection to **others** by rating this on a seven-point scale, from 'never' to 'always', and writing that number in the box. On the scale, a score of 1 indicates 'Never appropriate', 4 indicates 'Sometimes appropriate' and 7 indicates 'Always appropriate'.

a) How appropriate is the amount of affection he or she shows others?

Consider how appropriate you find the **amount** of affection your child shows to **others** by giving a rating on the seven-point scale, where 1 indicates 'Not enough', 4 indicates 'About right' and 7 indicates 'Too much'.

✓

Please see the example below:

1. Is your child able to say 'hello' to others in an appropriate manner? ☐ 1

For example, rating this as a '1' means that you consider your child is rarely appropriate when saying 'hello' to others because he or she does not do it enough. Alternatively you may rate it as a '6' or '7' if the reason that your child was not able to say 'hello' in an appropriate manner was because he or she did it too frequently.

    a. What do you think of the amount he/she does this? ☐ 1

For example, rating this as a '1' means your child never says 'hello' in an appropriate manner, and may shout it at people or ignore people when a 'hello' would be appropriate.

There are 20 questions in this section.

The first 8 questions are about your child GIVING affection to **others**. Examples of 'others' are: school teachers, classmates, family friends, shopkeepers, and strangers.

GIVING VERBAL AFFECTION

1. Is your child able to say 'I love you/I like you' to others appropriately (e.g. classmates or family friends)? ☐

    a. What do you think of the amount he/she does this? ☐

2. Is your child able to say something to others about how important the relationship between them is appropriately? ☐

    a. What do you think of the amount he/she does this? ☐

3. Is your child able to compliment others in an appropriate way? ☐

    a. What do you think of the amount he/she does this? ☐

4. Is your child able to speak to others in an appropriately friendly manner? ☐

    a. What do you think of the amount he/she does this? ☐

GIVING PHYSICAL AFFECTION

5. Is your child able to hug others appropriately? ☐

    a. What do you think of the amount he/she does this? ☐

6. Is your child able to hold others' hands appropriately when he/she needs to (e.g. a school teacher)? ☐

    a. What do you think of the amount he/she does this? ☐

7. Is your child able to put his/her arm around the shoulder of others appropriately (e.g. classmates)? ☐

    a. What do you think of the amount he/she does this? ☐

8. Is your child able to physically acknowledge others appropriately, by giving them a touch on the arm, pat on the back, or similar? ☐

    a. What do you think of the amount he/she does this? ☐

✠ ✠ ✠

The next 8 questions are about your child accepting and RECEIVING affection from **others**.

RECEIVING VERBAL AFFECTION

9. Is your child able to respond appropriately to others saying 'I like you/I love you' to him/her (e.g. classmates)? ☐

    a. What do you think of the amount he/she does this? ☐

10. Is your child able to respond to compliments from others? ☐

    a. What do you think of the amount he/she does this? ☐

11. Is your child able to accept thanks or praise from others appropriately? ☐

    a. What do you think of the amount he/she does this? ☐

12. Is your child able to speak in an appropriately friendly manner back to others when he/she is included in a conversation? ☐

    a. What do you think of the amount he/she does this? ☐

RECEIVING PHYSICAL AFFECTION

13. Is your child able to receive a hug from others appropriately (e.g. classmates or family friends)? ☐

    a. What do you think of the amount he/she does this? ☐

14. Is your child able to respond to a kiss from others appropriately (e.g. family friend)? ☐

    a. What do you think of the amount he/she does this? ☐

15. Is your child able to react appropriately when others touch him/her (e.g. classmates)? ☐

    a. What do you think of the amount he/she does this? ☐

16. Is your child able to react appropriately when others give him/her a pat on the back (e.g. classmates)? ☐

    a. What do you think of the amount he/she does this? ☐

✓

✠ ✠ ✠

The final 4 questions are about your child's ability to understand and share emotions with **others**.

COMMUNICATION OF EMPATHY

17. Is your child able to laugh appropriately with others? ☐

    a. What do you think of the amount he/she does this? ☐

18. Is your child able to show an appropriate level of interest in the actions and feelings of others? ☐

    a. What do you think of the amount he/she does this? ☐

19. Is your child able to be appropriately helpful to others? ☐

    a. What do you think of the amount he/she does this? ☐

20. Is your child able to smile at others appropriately? ☐

    a. What do you think of the amount he/she does this? ☐

✓

The Affection for You Questionnaire (AYQ)

The next questions are all to do with the types of affection your child (aged between 5 years and 13 years old) with autism spectrum disorder shows *you*. Please fill these questions out even if your child does not have any difficulty expressing affection to you.

There are two components to each question:

1. How often does your child show you that form of affection?

Consider how **often** your child shows affection to **you** by rating this on a seven-point scale, from 'never' to 'twice a day or more', and writing that number in the box. On the scale, a score of 1 = Never, 2 = Yearly, 3 = Monthly, 4 = Twice a week, 5 = Once a week, 6 = Once a day, 7 = Twice a day or more.

a) How appropriate is the amount of affection he or she shows you?

Consider the **amount** of affection your child shows **you** by giving a rating on the seven-point scale, where 1 indicates 'Not enough', 4 indicates 'About right' and 7 indicates 'Too much'.

✓

Please see the example below:

1. How often does he/she say 'hello' to you? $\boxed{6}$

For example, rating this as a '6' indicates that your child says 'hello' to you once a day on average.

    a. What do you think of the amount he/she does this? $\boxed{4}$

For example, rating this as a '4' means that you consider your child saying 'hello' to you once a day to be about the 'right' amount.

There are 19 questions in this section.

The first 9 questions are about your child GIVING affection to **you**. Please consider how often he/she does this as well as how satisfied you are with this amount.

GIVING VERBAL AFFECTION

1. How often does he/she say 'I love you' to *you*? ☐

    a. What do you think of the amount he/she does this? ☐

2. How often does he/she say something to *you* about how important your relationship is to him/her? ☐

    a. What do you think of the amount he/she does this? ☐

3. How often does he/she thank *you*? ☐

    a. What do you think of the amount he/she does this? ☐

4. How often does he/she speak to *you* in a friendly manner? ☐

    a. What do you think of the amount he/she does this? ☐

GIVING PHYSICAL AFFECTION

5. How often does he/she come up and hug *you*? ☐

    a. What do you think of the amount he/she does this? ☐

6. How often does he/she want to hold *your* hand? ☐

    a. What do you think of the amount he/she does this? ☐

7. How often does he/she want to sit close to *you*? ☐

    a. What do you think of the amount he/she does this? ☐

8. How often does he/she put his/her arm around *your* shoulder, around your waist, or around your legs? ☐

    a. What do you think of the amount he/she does this? ☐

9. How often does he/she acknowledge *your* presence by touching you in some way, e.g. a pat on the back or arm, a touch on the hand, or similar? ☐

    a. What do you think of the amount he/she does this? ☐

✠ ✠ ✠

The next 6 questions are about your child accepting and RECEIVING affection from **you**.

RECEIVING VERBAL AFFECTION

10. How often does he/she say 'I love you' back to *you*? ☐

    a. What do you think of the amount he/she does this? ☐

11. How often does he/she respond with pleasure to *you* using a pet name or term of endearment to refer to him/her? □

    a. What do you think of the amount he/she does this? □

12. How often does he/she speak in a friendly manner back to *you*? □

    a. What do you think of the amount she/she does this? □

RECEIVING PHYSICAL AFFECTION

13. How often does he/she enjoy it when *you* hug him/her? □

    a. What do you think of the amount he/she does this? □

14. How often does he/she enjoy it when *you* kiss him/her? □

    a. What do you think of the amount he/she does this? □

15. How often does he/she hold hands with you when *you* ask him/her to? □

    a. What do you think of the amount he/she does this? □

✠ ✠ ✠

The final 4 questions are about your child's ability to understand and share emotions with **you**.

COMMUNICATION OF EMPATHY

16. How often does he/she laugh with *you*?

☐

    a.   What do you think of the amount he/she does this?

☐

17. How often does he/she show an interest in what *you* are doing or feeling?

☐

    a.   What do you think of the amount he/she does this?

☐

18. How often is he/she helpful when *you* need it?

☐

    a.   What do you think of the amount he/she does this?

☐

19. How often does he/she smile at *you* with happiness?

☐

    a.   What do you think of the amount he/she does this?

☐

The General Affection Questionnaire (GAQ)

Please answer the following questions about your child by writing a number in the box, which shows your level of agreement with the 12 statements. On the scale, a score of 1 indicates 'Strongly disagree' and 7 indicates 'Strongly agree'.

1. He/she has only a limited number of ways of expressing affection. ☐

2. He/she shows a lack of affection. ☐

3. He/she has difficulties initiating affection. ☐

4. He/she finds it difficult receiving affection from others. ☐

5. He/she uses inappropriate expressions of affection. ☐

6. I have had to spend time teaching him/her about affection. ☐

7. There seems to be a difference between his/her physical need for touch and his/her desire to express affection. ☐

8. He/she has difficulties with affection and these interfere with school. ☐

9. He/she has difficulties with affection that cause problems with his/her siblings. ☐

10. He/she has difficulties displaying affection to those outside of our immediate family. ☐

✓

11. He/she has quirky or unusual ways of giving or wanting to receive affection. ☐

12. He/she has difficulties understanding that certain types and levels of affection are not appropriate to show to everyone (e.g. does not discriminate well between those who it is appropriate to hug/kiss/touch). ☐